EARTHQUAKES

DANIEL ROGERS

HODDER
Wayland

an imprint of Hodder Children's Books

GEOGRAPHY STARTS HERE!

Earthquakes

OTHER TITLES IN THE SERIES
Hills and Mountains · Maps and Symbols
Rivers and Streams · Volcanoes
Weather Around You · Where People Live
Your Environment

Produced for Wayland Publishers Limited by
Roger Coote Publishing
Gissing's Farm
Fressingfield
Suffolk IP21 5SH

Designer: Victoria Webb

Editor: Alex Edmonds

Picture Research: Lynda Lines

Illustrations: Peter Bull and Tony Townsend

First published in Great Britain in 1998
by Wayland Publishers Ltd

Reprinted in 2002 by Hodder Wayland,
an imprint of Hodder Children's Books

© Hodder Wayland 1998

British Library Cataloguing in Publication Data

Rogers, Daniel, 1955–

Earthquakes. – (Geography starts here!)

1.Earthquakes – Juvenile literature

I.Title

551.2'2

ISBN 07502 4155 1
Printed and bound in Hong Kong

All Wayland books encourage children to read and help them improve their literacy.

✓ The contents page, page numbers, headings and index help locate specific pieces of information.

✓ The glossary reinforces alphabetic knowledge and extends vocabulary.

✓ The further information section suggests other books dealing with the same subject.

Picture Acknowledgements

Page 1: Rex/Novedades/Sipa. 4: Rex/Rasmussen/Sipa. 5: FLPA/Steve McCutcheon. 7: Rex. 8: Rex/Butler/Baue. 9: Vinay Parelkas/Dinodia/OSF. 11: Photri. 12: Rex/Vladimir Sichov/Sipa. 13: Getty Images/Paul Chesley. 14: FLPA/Steve McCutcheon. 16: Associated Press/Katsumi Kasahara. 17: Topham/AP. 18: Warren Faidley/OSF. 19: Getty Images/Leverett Bradley. 20: Rex/Today. 21, 22: Rex/Sipa. 23: Rex/Gropp/Sipa. 25: Photri. 27: Science Photo Library/David Parker. 28: Photri/NASA. 29: Science Photo Library/David Parker. Cover: Rex/Iwasa/Sipa.

The photo on the previous page shows people being rescued after an earthquake in Mexico City in 1985.

CONTENTS

EARTH-SHATTERING

When an earthquake happens, the ground may start to rumble and shake. The shaking often lasts for only a few seconds, but it can cause terrible damage.

Each year there are more than a million earthquakes. Most of them are too small to notice. Others cause a little damage. Only a few earthquakes are big enough to bring death and great destruction.

People rescue their belongings from their shattered homes after an earthquake in San Francisco, USA, in 1989.

An earthquake has cracked open this road in Alaska, USA.

THE WORLD'S EARTHQUAKES

The Earth's surface layer, or crust, is made up of pieces called plates. Although the plates are made of solid rock they are not fixed in one place – they are moving all the time.

The plates move because they are floating on hot, melted rocks in a layer called the mantle, beneath the Earth's crust.

Most earthquakes happen where two of the Earth's plates meet. In 1998 two strong earthquakes hit Afghanistan, causing terrible damage.

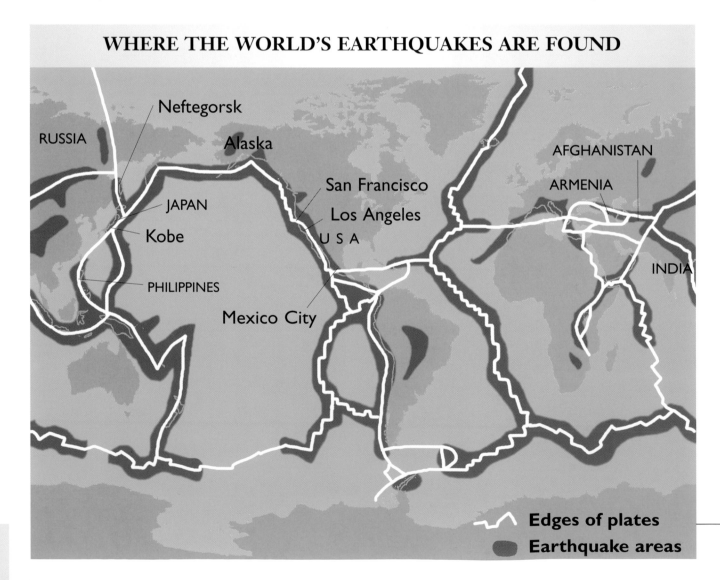

WHERE THE WORLD'S EARTHQUAKES ARE FOUND

Neftegorsk

RUSSIA

Alaska

AFGHANISTAN

San Francisco

ARMENIA

JAPAN

Los Angeles

Kobe

U S A

INDIA

PHILIPPINES

Mexico City

⌒ **Edges of plates**

● **Earthquake areas**

This railway bridge in Kobe, Japan, was destroyed by an earthquake in 1995.

WHEN THE GROUND SHAKES

Being in a strong earthquake is terrifying. First, there is a loud, deep rumbling sound. Then the ground begins to shake and crack open. Sometimes it moves up and down in waves, like ripples on a pond.

Buildings, bridges and some roads are rocked and shaken until they collapse. People have to run for their lives.

This road crashed down on top of another during the 1994 earthquake in Los Angeles, USA.

These buildings were turned to rubble by an earthquake in Maharashtra, India, in 1993.

What Causes an Earthquake?

Where the Earth's plates push together, the rocks do not always slide past each other smoothly. Sometimes they get stuck. The forces pushing them build up until something has to give.

This diagram shows how the rocks move along a fault in an earthquake.

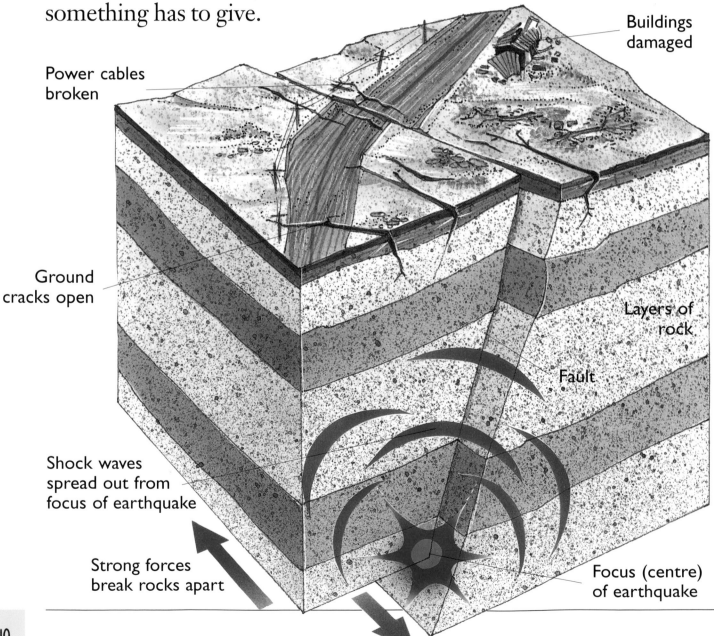

Buildings damaged

Power cables broken

Ground cracks open

Layers of rock

Fault

Shock waves spread out from focus of earthquake

Strong forces break rocks apart

Focus (centre) of earthquake

FEEL THE FORCE

Put the palm of your hand on a smooth tabletop and press down. As you push down, try to slide your hand forwards along the table. Does it slide smoothly, or jerk suddenly and then stop again? Imagine your hand and the table are rocks pushing against each other. Do you see now how an earthquake starts?

This man in California, USA, is measuring how far the road has moved in an earthquake.

Suddenly, the rocks break apart with a huge jolt that sets off an earthquake. Earthquakes usually happen deep underground, but they send out strong shock waves in all directions. Some of these shock waves reach the surface and make the ground shake.

The Power of Earthquakes

Some earthquakes are much stronger than others. The strength of an earthquake is measured using the Richter Scale. An earthquake measuring 2 or less on the Richter Scale is too weak to feel. Earthquakes of 7 or more are extremely powerful and can cause great damage.

The earthquake that struck Kobe, Japan, in 1995 measured 7.2 on the Richter Scale.

This man is testing a concrete wall to see how badly it would be damaged if an earthquake struck.

Another way of measuring earthquakes is the Mercalli Scale. This scale measures how much an earthquake shakes objects and the damage it causes to buildings.

These homes in Anchorage, Alaska, were destroyed by a landslide following a very strong earthquake.

After an Earthquake

In mountain areas, earthquakes can set off avalanches, landslides and mudslides, as huge amounts of snow, rock or mud are loosened by the shaking. They slide down the sides of the mountains, flattening everything in their way.

After a big earthquake, there may be smaller earthquakes, called aftershocks. Sometimes they knock down weakened buildings.

Landslides, mudslides and avalanches can rush downhill very fast. They destroy buildings and crops in their path.

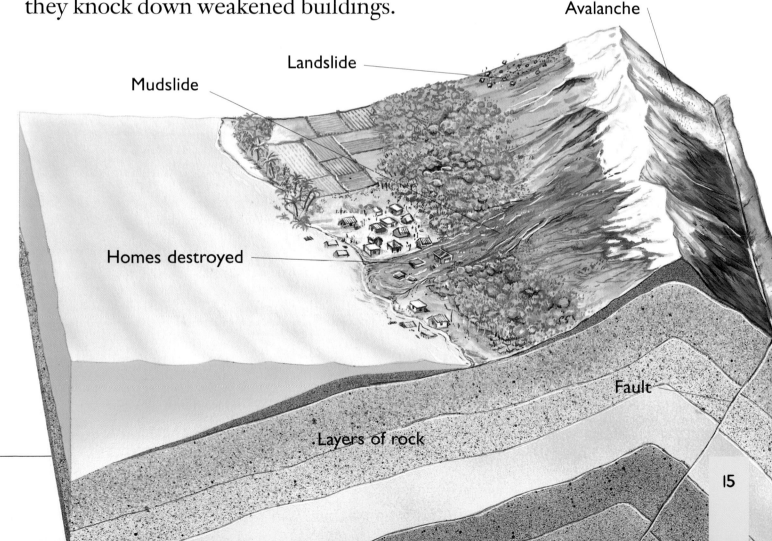

Avalanche

Landslide

Mudslide

Homes destroyed

Fault

Layers of rock

Tsunamis

Earthquakes under the ocean or near the coast can cause huge waves, called tsunamis. These waves can sweep across the ocean at up to 800 kilometres per hour.

This harbour on Okushiri Island, Japan, was destroyed by a tsunami in 1993.

A man tries to save some of his possessions after a tsunami flattened his home in the Philippines.

In the open ocean, a tsunami may be only a metre high. But by the time it reaches land, it can grow to more than 30 metres. When this huge wall of water bursts ashore, it can cause terrible damage.

PEOPLE AND EARTHQUAKES

A powerful earthquake can have a terrible effect on people's lives. Their homes, schools, hospitals, factories and offices may be flattened. Roads and bridges may be too damaged to use.

Water pipes, power lines and gas pipes may be broken. Fires can sweep through a shattered city. They may burn the buildings that were left standing after the earthquake.

An earthquake in California, USA, has knocked down power cables and started fires.

This block of flats in Los Angeles, USA, was so badly damaged by an earthquake that it had to be knocked down.

Killer Quakes

In an area where there are villages, towns and cities, a big earthquake can kill thousands of people. Many victims are crushed or buried when buildings collapse.

These people survived an earthquake in Armenia in 1988.

In 1985, a huge earthquake in Mexico City killed over 7,000 people.

Avalanches and mudslides can destroy whole cities, killing many of the people who live there. Tsunamis flood the land. Many people may drown and crops are ruined.

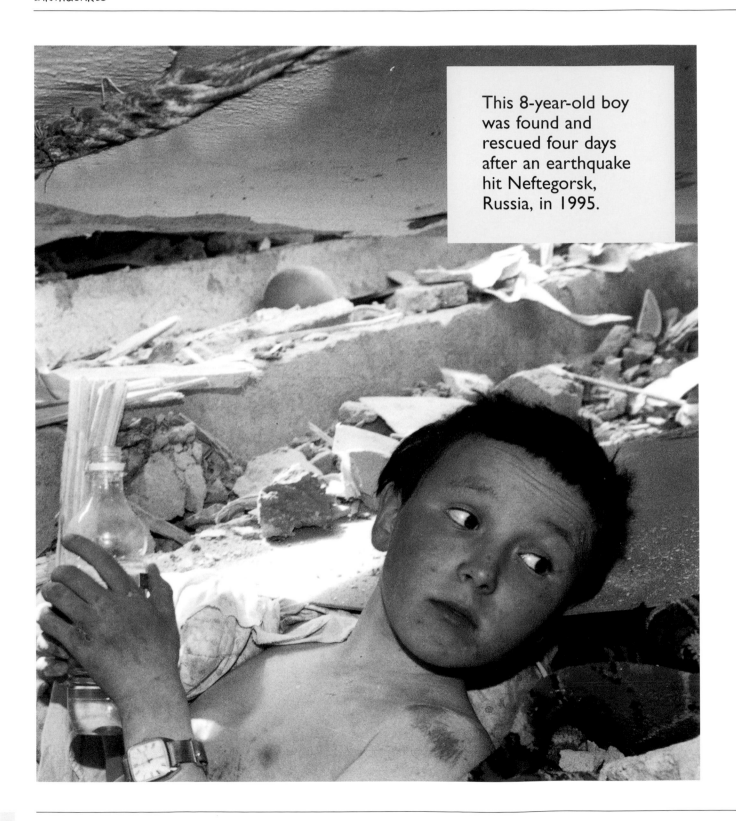

This 8-year-old boy was found and rescued four days after an earthquake hit Neftegorsk, Russia, in 1995.

Earthquake Rescue

After a major earthquake, help is needed urgently. People who are trapped under collapsed buildings must be found and rescued quickly. Injured people need to be treated.

Food, clean water, blankets and shelter have to be brought in. Then power and water supplies must be repaired.

These people's homes were destroyed by an earthquake. Rescue workers have given them tents and blankets.

Lives on the Line

In 1906 a huge earthquake and fire destroyed San Francisco in the USA, killing over 500 people. In 1989, another earthquake struck. Over 27,000 homes were wrecked and 62 people died.

Millions of people still live in San Francisco, even though they know there will be more earthquakes in the future.

GET THE SHAKES

Imagine you live in an earthquake zone. Get together with your friends and act out what you would do if an earthquake struck.

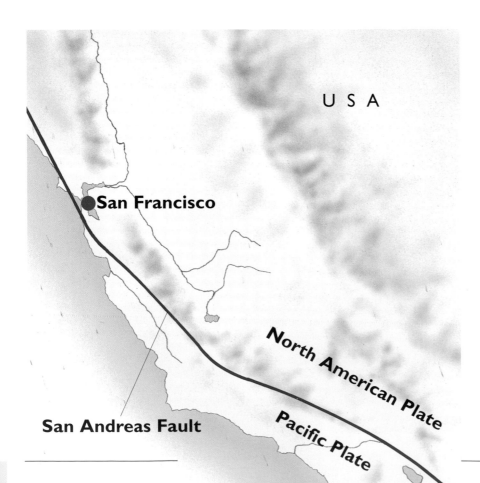

San Francisco suffers earthquakes because the city is on the San Andreas Fault, where two of the Earth's plates meet.

People in Mexico were able to read about the earthquake that hit their city, just 30 minutes after it happened.

Some places, such as Japan, suffer many earthquakes. Each time, people rebuild their damaged homes and carry on with their lives.

CUTTING THE RISK

We can't stop earthquakes happening. But we can try to stop them causing so much destruction. One way is to make buildings that don't collapse in an earthquake.

New buildings must be built so that they don't sink into the ground or topple over. Buildings must also be able to sway from side to side during an earthquake, without breaking apart.

In some places where there are many earthquakes, new buildings have to be made earthquake-proof.

Normal building

Building shakes

Building breaks apart

People injured or killed

Built on a solid base

Earthquake-proof building

Building sways gently

No damage to building

People safe

Built on rubber springs

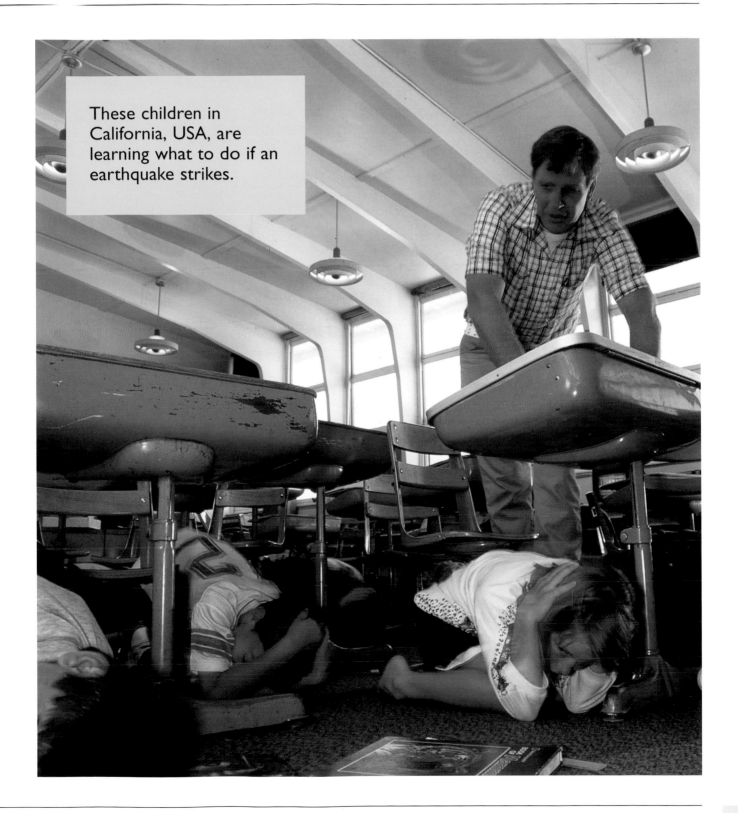

These children in California, USA, are learning what to do if an earthquake strikes.

Predicting Earthquakes

If we knew when earthquakes were about to happen, people could be moved to safety. Scientists try to predict earthquakes using equipment that measures movements in the Earth's rocks. But they don't always get it right.

Animals may give us warning signs, too. People have noticed that when an earthquake is coming, animals seem to get very restless and even leave the area.

Scientists work on equipment that will help to predict earthquakes.

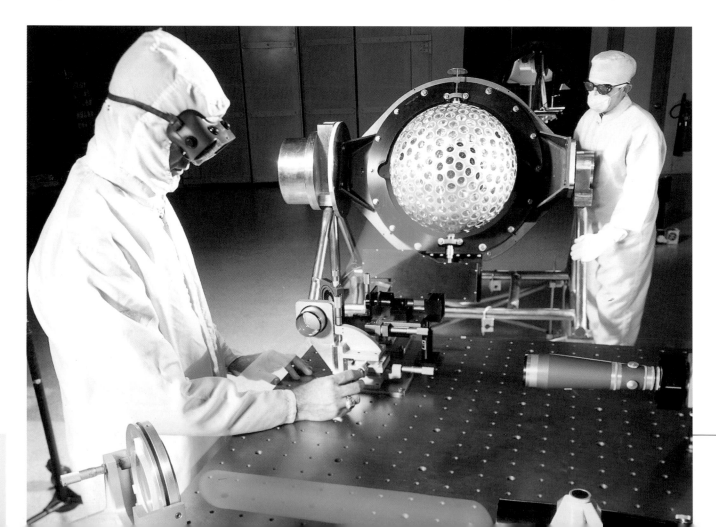

This man is checking equipment that is used to measure movement in the Earth's rocks.

EARTHQUAKE FACTS AND FIGURES

The deadliest earthquakes

When a massive earthquake struck Shensi province, China, in 1556, about 830,000 people were killed. The worst earthquake disaster in recent times was also in China. It happened in Tangshan province in 1976. It measured 7.9 on the Richter Scale, and about 750,000 people died.

The greatest destruction

The most damage caused by an earthquake was in the cities of Tokyo and Yokohama, Japan, in 1923. Around 575,000 homes were destroyed by the earthquake, which measured 8.2 on the Richter Scale.

The worst avalanche

When an earthquake struck the mountainous region of Huascarán, Peru, in 1970, it set off a huge avalanche. An 80-metre-high wave of ice, mud and rock hurtled down the mountains at 400 kilometres per hour. It struck Yungay, killing over 18,000 people there.

The worst landslide

In 1920, an earthquake caused a landslide in Kansu province, China. About 200,000 people were killed.

The highest tsunami

The biggest tsunami ever caused by an earthquake under the sea was seen off Ishigaki Island, Japan, in 1771. It was estimated to be 85 metres high – about the same as a 25-storey building.

The Richter Scale

This scale is used to measure the strength of earthquakes. There is no limit to how high an earthquake can measure on the Richter Scale, but the strongest quakes ever were 8.6.

The Mercalli Scale

There are 12 levels:
1 Earthquake not felt.
2 Felt slightly in upper floors of buildings.
3 Hanging objects swing.
4 Strong vibration; cars rock from side to side.
5 Felt strongly; doors swing.
6 Books fall from shelves; furniture moves; trees shake.
7 Difficult to stand up; furniture breaks; plaster falls.
8 Chimneys and walls collapse.
9 Ground cracks; underground pipes break; many buildings fall.
10 Most buildings collapse; large landslides.
11 Railway lines badly bent; underground pipes wrecked.
12 Total destruction.

Further Reading

The Violent Earth CD-ROM by Sally Morgan (Wayland, 1995)

Earthquakes, Closer Look At series, by Joyce Pope (Watts, 1996)

Earthquake, Violent Earth series, by John Dudman (Wayland, 1992)

Earthquakes, First Starts series, by Keith Lye (Watts, 1992)

Earthquakes, Project Homework series, by Jane Walker (Watts, 1997)

Volcano, Earthquake and Hurricane, Quest! series, by Nick Arnold (Wayland, 1996)

Volcanoes and Earthquakes, Restless Earth series, by Terry Jennings (Belitha Press, 1998)

The Power of Earthquakes, Natural Disasters series, by Susan Bullen (Wayland, 1994)

GLOSSARY

Aftershocks Small earthquakes that happen after the main earthquake.

Avalanches Masses of snow and ice that fall down the sides of mountains when they are loosened by a jolt, such as an earthquake.

Crust The surface layer of the Earth.

Fault A deep crack in the Earth's surface where the rocks have split apart.

Focus The place underground where an earthquake starts.

Landslides Masses of rocks and soil falling down mountains.

Mercalli Scale A way of measuring how much damage an earthquake has caused.

Mudslides Masses of mud sliding down the sides of mountains.

Plates Large pieces of rock that make up the Earth's crust.

Restless Worried or unable to stay still.

Richter Scale A way of measuring how strong an earthquake was.

Rubble Pieces of broken stone, concrete and bricks from buildings that have fallen down.

Starvation Not having enough food to eat.

Tsunami An enormous wave caused by a big volcanic explosion or by an underwater earthquake.

This road near Los Angeles, USA, collapsed in an earthquake. Repairing damaged buildings and roads costs an enormous amount of money.

Hwy ↗

31

INDEX